Helping wildlife begins in your garden

Contents

Wildlife can provide a source of endless fascination in a garden. Watching birds, butterflies, even bats and hedgehogs make themselves at home is something that gardeners of all ages can enjoy. What's more, certain types of wildlife play an important role in the garden by helping to control pests, meaning you do not need to resort to harmful artificial methods. And at a time when many wild species are threatened by the loss of natural habitats, your wildlife garden can help to redress the balance and ensure their survival for generations to come. This book gives clear and practical advice on how to create a wildlife haven in your back garden, and how to enjoy it through the changing seasons.

1

The wildlife garden: planning for success

Why **attract wildlife?**

Wildlife is seemingly on the decline everywhere. Mechanized farming, widespread pesticide spraying and modern changes in land use and management have all been blamed. Traditionally the countryside was seen as the place to watch nature, while the garden was for flowers and veg. This view is changing; more and more gardeners are now sharing their herbaceous borders with wildlife of all sizes.

There are a vast number of fascinating creatures to see in the garden and each adds to the pleasure we get from our surroundings. The antics of a gang of noisy sparrows in a small bush may be commonplace, but they are

A vast number of fascinating creatures will visit or live in your garden if you plan and plant for wildlife. Above left, goldfinch and right, the speckled wood butterfly.

always amusing; but then there is nothing more thrilling than seeing some strange new bird or unidentified butterfly making itself at home on your very doorstep. Every little bit we do in our own plots of land will help bolster the broader effort of nationwide nature conservation.

In major cities, gardens make up a significant part of the land area (20% of all open space in London is private garden for example). Some are intricately manicured, some are left to rack and ruin by disinterested owners. There are endless sheltered corners behind hedge and fence; there are trees, shrubs and flowers of all kinds; there are banks and hollows, ponds and ditches, log piles and compost bins aplenty. It is this patchwork of different plots that creates the perfect varied habitat for a wide diversity of wildlife.

A patchwork of varied habitats will provide cover and food for numerous species and many of them are useful in the garden. Above: The common toad (left) and the hedgehog (right), both consumers of slugs and snails.

What makes a **successful wildlife** garden?

Space and time

You don't need a total garden make-over to attract wildlife, large and small; nor do you need several acres, paid staff, or an unmanageable commitment in your gardening time. All that is required is a change of mind-set, a sympathetic approach to wildlife and an acceptance that nature is not always neat and tidy.

Sound **planning**

A first step is to make a map of your existing garden. It can be very sketchy or precisely measured, as long as it gives you an idea of the space available and what might fit where. If you are more artistically gifted, you could even make a perspective drawing and try superimposing new features on it. In addition, there are many books that provide advice on garden design and planning and also a range of garden design software products.

An important decision will be whether you set aside one particular area for wildlife, or incorporate wildlife-friendly features throughout. If you have a naturalistic hedge boundary already, for example, you could make that edge of the garden wild, while making the remainder more formal. Remember, every little helps.

Before you take any action use this book to help you decide upon what sort of wildlife garden you want.

Gardening **for wildlife** – the **basics**

- Wildlife needs food, water, shelter and places to breed.

- Native wildlife thrives best on native plants (including 'weeds').

- Attract wildlife variety by a varied planting of low/medium/tall climbing plants.

- Avoid chemicals: sprays, powders and pellets.

- Don't over-fertilize the soil.

- Don't be too tidy.

- Watch, learn and enjoy.

action stations

1 **Decide** whether you will set aside one particular area for wildlife or, whether to incorporate wildlife-friendly features throughout your garden.

2 **Plan:** Make a map of your existing garden and plan what wildlife features can go where.

3 **Think** about what wildlife needs and which wildlife you primarily want to attract; then plan for features that will provide food, shelter and places to breed.

4 **Remember** that nature is not always tidy. Log piles, compost bins and undisturbed areas will provide food and shelter.

Creating your wildlife garden

Starting **from scratch**

Before you start to plan your new garden, take a look at any more 'natural' parts of your local neighbourhood – nearby countryside, railway embankments, overgrown gardens, nature parks. These will give you a good idea what plants will flourish in your own wildlife garden depending on your local soil geology, sunshine hours, wind and rainfall.

New gardens – blank canvases

When planning a new garden the first thing to think out is how it will all work. Where will children or pets play? Where will paths lead? Will you have a patio or a barbecue area? Do you want a working vegetable patch, soft fruit cage or herb garden? These are the parts

Take a look at the more natural parts of your neighbourhood to give you an idea of what plants will work in your garden.

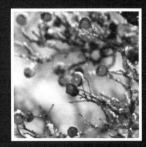

of the garden that you will occupy most and therefore where you will most often disturb wildlife. When you have sorted out where these are going to go, you will know where there can be quiet corners and wild places.

Sunlight

How the sunlight moves across the garden during the day will be a key part in your decision making. A natural sun-trap might dictate where you build a patio or place a bench, or where you might put particularly sun-loving plants. A shady area might be suitable for woodland glade plants, a fern garden, a log pile or for hiding your garden shed.

Contours

What are the levels like? Are there natural banks, dips or slopes that can be used to give the garden variety? Are parts of the garden naturally drier or wetter than elsewhere? Is there a place for a pond?

First impressions

When you enter the garden and as you walk through it, what views or vistas will greet you? First impressions are very important. When you are in the garden, looking round at your house and neighbouring buildings, are there views you want to block for the sake of privacy? Are there things you want to hide for the sake of aesthetics?

Last resort

Don't use herbicide to clear an area, unless you are using it in conjunction with mechanical clearance of truly invasive and difficult plants like Japanese knot-weed and Russian vine.

Most unwanted plants can be cut or pulled manually. If you must, use spot herbicides on individual plants.

Existing gardens – adapt and change

Taking over an existing garden does not mean that you have to keep it all. But equally it does not mean you need to tear it all out. Tastes differ, and you may have ideas about what you do or don't like. Spend some time thinking about what an existing garden already has and what benefit to wildlife it can make. What trees do the birds forage in most? Where do butterflies often sun themselves? What flowers are already dripping with bees and hoverflies?

There is no hurry and seeing the garden through several months you may change your mind more than once. Use the same garden-from-scratch criteria listed above to think how an existing garden might be modified, but act conservatively – if you do a little first, you can do a little more later.

Mature gardens – seeing the light

Established gardens offer shade, important for a calm seating area, and for woodland glade plants. But if trees and shrubs are too dense, they block out the light. Opening up dense trees and scrub will have immediate benefits for the ground flora beneath, but before you cut down, check exactly where the sunlight will fall and what view, if any, is exposed to neighbouring buildings. Invasive trees like sycamore and ash should be thinned in preference to other native species like hawthorn, oak or beech. Non-native shrubs like snowberry, pyracantha and evergreen spindle can also be cleared without much ecological loss.

To tree or not to tree? – caution!

Large or old trees may have tree-preservation orders attached to them; check at your local council office before setting saw to wood. Taking out a small stem is one thing, lopping branches from large trees should only be done by a professional tree surgeon using the proper safety equipment.

A winter visitor, the redwing will feed in groups on berries such as hawthorn and rowan.

▌Habitats

A good mixture of habitats will help to improve the diversity of wildlife attracted and supported by your garden. The more variety you have in habitats, the greater the variety of the wildlife colonizing. And the closer these habitats are to nature, the better they will work.

Grass: Green deserts and wildflower meadows

A lush lawn, with alternating parallel lines of dark and light, created by carefully aligned mowing, may look attractive on the bowling green, but it could be no more than a green desert as far as wildlife is concerned. Relax the mowing regime and small but significant changes will occur. Raise the cutting blades of the lawn-mower, mow less often and clear away all the grass cuttings (don't use a hover-mower that mulches the cuttings back into the turf). Any plants already in the lawn will now have a chance to flower occasionally.

Many native butterflies have caterpillars that feed on grass, but not in the short sward of a lawn. Try leaving an area to grow long. Either cut it once a year, in August (traditional hay-cutting time), or in June and September. Grass flowers may be small, but the swaying heads are very pretty and attract small hoverflies that feed on the pollen. Always remove the grass

cuttings; mulching them into the turf, fertilizes the soil and encourages only the tougher rank species like rye, at the expense of more attractive and delicate species of grass.

Butterfly grasses. Caterpillars of large, small and Essex skippers, wall brown, speckled wood, meadow brown, gatekeeper and small heath butterflies feed on cock's-foot grass *Dactylis glomerata,* Yorkshire fog *Holcus lanatus*, timothy *Phleum pratense*, false brome *Brachypodium sylvaticum*, meadow grasses *Poa* species, bent grasses *Agrostis* species and fescues *Festuca* species. None of them favour the rye grasses *Lolium* species used in lawn seed mixtures and commercial turf!

True wildflower meadows are an attractive idea, but can be difficult to achieve. A well-fertilized soil soon allows dominant grasses to edge out

Relaxing the mowing regime and setting aside an area for grasses will help to provide habitat for hoverflies, bees and butterflies.

delicate seedlings. Unless you are prepared to scour away the topsoil your best bet is to use potted plants plugged into the turf (though this can be expensive) or plant up a wildflower border nearby. Never dig up wild flowers from the countryside though, it is illegal and they rarely survive the translocation. There are plenty of proprietary seed mixes on the market, but for best results choose one that is locally, or at least nationally harvested and does not include imported seeds.

Planting for **diversity**

The standard gardening doctrine of putting low plants at the front, intermediate plants in the middle and tall plants at the back also applies to a wildlife garden. Diversity of plant architecture increases the diversity of micro-habitats and niches into which wildlife will be attracted.

The very lowest plants will be the close-cut grass of the lawn, but any corners allowed to be unmown or only mown irregularly encourage daisies and buttercups in their midst. Moving into the edge of the borders, small compact plants such as candytuft, lady's smock, and borage will attract bees and butterflies to their nectar-rich flowers.

Further back Michaelmas daisy, lavender, globe thistle, pink valerian and rocket form a middle-ground range of colour and scent. And at the back tall

Female blackcap on blackberry.

stems of golden rod, honesty, yellow loosestrife, hollyhock and millet provide spikes of nectar- and seed-bearing flowers. These then lead into shrubs such as hawthorn, elder and sallow, and maybe even to trees beyond.

The importance of a varied plant architecture lies in its creation of a gently undulating edge from the ground zero of mown lawn to the hidden tree tops. Perches for birds and dragonflies, guy-lines for spider webs, sunny leaves for basking butterflies, sweet-smelling flowers for bees and hoverflies blend together in a continuous patchwork of microhabitats.

Shelter

To encourage wildlife to stay in the garden, once it has been attracted, it must be given somewhere to shelter – during the night, during poor weather and during the winter.

Log-on

A small log pile tucked into a shady corner will provide a hiding place for frogs, toads, voles and countless insects. Don't stack it too tightly or too neatly, and make sure it will not be disturbed. If you half bury the bottom logs in the soil, you may also encourage rotten-wood creatures like stag beetles. On the other hand, if you already have a working woodpile, for a stove or open fires indoors, you should discourage anything taking up residence. It will only be disturbed at the worst possible time, during winter when you are stoking up the fire. Stack the logs tight and regular, preferably on a solid base, and under cover.

Bin it

Compost bins attract slow-worms, grass-snakes and small mammals, particularly if natural decomposition and fermentation warms the compost. Avoid mixing or disturbing the compost during the winter months.

Leave well alone

A pile of dried leaves at the bottom of a hedge is a perfect nest for a hiding hedgehog. A wooden trellis planted with small shrubs and climbers is just as good as a hedge and also has the benefit of creating a screen or partition in the garden – a good way of hiding an ugly shed or the dustbins.

Climbing

Ivy, clematis or other climbers soon accumulate a natural thicket of twigs, dead leaves and other debris amongst their twisting stems. Do any pruning in late summer or the following spring to minimize disturbance.

Put in a **pond?**

Water will immediately attract wildlife, either to live in it or to drink and bathe. Choose a sunny open spot, not overhung by trees or bushes, but with a hedge or fence nearby to offer some shelter. Using a flexible plastic or butyl (rubber) liner is the easiest means of construction, or if space is very tight a pre-formed plastic pond.

When digging the hole use gentle slopes around the edge to allow animals to climb in and out easily. Make steps or shelves at various levels in the pond to accommodate a variety of plant types. Have at least one deep area (more than 60cm); this will act like a temperature buffer and remain cool if the shallows get lots of sun, and it will not freeze if the surface of the pond ices over.

It is important to protect the liner from puncture by any sharp stones in the soil. Line the hole with sand and use old carpet or fibre matting as an extra cushion layer underneath a butyl sheet. Fill it with tap water before you trim the liner edges and bury them or disguise with turf, rocks or logs. Allow 48 hours for any chlorine to dissipate before you add any plants or animals.

Pond plants fit roughly into three broad categories and you will need some of each to make your pond as wildlife-friendly as possible. Native species are ideal because they are already acclimatized and are less likely to become invasive.

- In **deep water** sink submerged plants such as: water starwort *Callitriche stagnalis*, hornwort *Ceratophylum demersum*, water milfoil *Myriophyllum spicatum*, curly pondweed *Potamogeton crispus*, canadian pondweed *Elodea canadensis*.

- For **intermediate depths** use floating plants such as: waterlilies yellow *Nuphar lutea* and white *Nymphaea alba*, water soldier *Stratiotes aloides*, arrowhead *Sagittaria sagittifolia*, broad-leaf pondweed *Potamogeton natans*, water crowfoot *Ranunculus aquatilis*, amphibious bistort *Polygonum amphibium*.

- Around the **shallow edges** of the pond and out into any surrounding boggy areas use marginal plants: water mint *Mentha aquatica*, yellow flag iris *Iris pseudacorus*, water plantain *Alisma plantago-aquatica*, brooklime

Veronica beccabunga, flowering rush *Butomus umbellatus*, greater spearwort *Ranunculus lingua* and reedmace *Typha latifolia*.

Aim for two-thirds of the pond with plant cover and one-third left as open water. If you inoculate your pool with a bucket of water collected from a mature pond, you will introduce many invertebrates including water fleas, Daphnia species, which help clear the green soup-like appearance of microscopic algal blooms.

It is usually acceptable to introduce frog or toad spawn from a neighbour's pond, but if you want a truly wildlife-friendly pond do not stock it with fish, they will eat everything else. Even small native fish like sticklebacks are fierce hunters and will strip a pond of tadpoles, boatmen, beetles and dragonfly larvae.

For more information read '*Create ponds*', in the Green Essentials series.

Putting in a pond is one of the most effective methods of attracting wildlife.

habitat catalogue

- **Borders** – Choose a mixture of seeds, bedding and established plants for immediate effect.

- **Grass** – If establishing a new lawn, seeds provide an opportunity for a more sympathetic mixture of species. Ease the mowing regime and remove grass cuttings. Alternatively, set-aside an area for wild flowers and grasses.

- **Hedges** – Use traditional hedgerow species such as hawthorn, blackthorn, hazel, holly, beech, lime, viburnum, spindle, privet and yew.

- **Log piles** – Keep unwanted wood from felled trees and lopped branches. Stack irregularly for shelter and fungus-feeders.

- **Shade and glades** – Use the variety of sunny and shady areas to encourage sun-loving or woodland glade plants.

- **Shrubs** – Plant them where they will have room to expand.

- **Trees** – Plant native species like birch, rowan and wild cherry to attract wildlife and let in light. Avoid fast-growing species such as ash, sycamore and Leyland Cyprus.

- **Trellis and fences** – A trellis or fence planted with climbers provides effective wildlife friendly shelter and screening.

- **Water** – A pond or even a half-barrel will attract aquatic insects to breed and birds to drink.

action stations

1 **Find out** what will grow best, by looking at nearby nature sites, other gardens and the surrounding countryside.

2 **Create** a variety of habitats to encourage a greater variety of wildlife.

3 **Shelter** is as important as food and drink, so think about a log pile and other undisturbed places.

4 **Put in a pond** to encourage aquatic wildlife and as a place for birds and animals to drink.

5 **Existing gardens:** Spend some time thinking about what an existing garden already has and what benefit to wildlife it can make.

6 **Mature gardens:** If trees and shrubs are too dense, selective thinning out will provide immediate benefits for ground flora.

3

Food, drink and shelter

Food and drink

As well as being colourful ornaments, flowers offer the key attractions to wildlife – nectar, pollen, seeds and berries. Butterflies, moths, bees and hoverflies come for nectar and pollen, while later in the year birds will eagerly peck out the seeds and berries.

There are hundreds of plants to choose from and they can vary from region to region. Check out your local nursery for the many plants or seed mixes that are now often specially highlighted as being wildlife-friendly. To get you started here are our top ten nectar and top ten seed and berry plants. Ask for them at your local nursery or garden centre.

top ten
nectar plants

- **Borage** *Borago officinalis*
- **Candytuft** *Iberis matronalis*
- **Honeysuckle** *Lonicera periclymenum* (for moths at dusk)
- **Mallow** several *Malva* and *Lavatera* species
- **Marjorum** *Origanum vulgare* (also use leaves for cooking)
- **Mignonette** *Reseda odorata*
- **Mint** several *Mentha* species
- **Orpine (ice-plant)** *Sedum spectabile*
- **Scabious** *Scabiosa atropurpurea*
- **Valerian** *Centranthus ruber*

Note: *Avoid* the butterfly-bush, *Buddleja davidii*, unless you have a very large garden. It does attract bees and butterflies, but is very vigorous and invasive. Ivy, *Hedera helix*, can be important in the autumn as one of the last nectar sources of the year.

top ten
seed & berry plants

- **Angelica** *Angelica archangelica*

- **Elder** *Sambucus nigra*

- **Globe thistle** *Echinops ritro*

- **Golden rod** *Solidago canadensis*

- **Hardhead** (knapweed) *Centaurea nigra*

- **Hawthorn** *Crataegus monogyna*

- **Honesty** *Lunaria biennis*

- **Meadowsweet** *Filipendula ulmaria*

- **Sunflower** many cultivars of *Helianthus annus*

- **Teasel** *Dipsacus follonum*

Planting to attract – hoverflies on hogweed.

Real food

Nectar and pollen may provide energy for adult insects, but it is during the caterpillar or grub stage that most of the eating and growing is done. And these are the favoured prey of many insect-eating birds. Flowers attract passing trade to stop and sip a while, but if you can encourage natural food plants in your garden you will be providing a year-round eatery and the basis of a self-sustained natural environment. Some of these will only be appropriate in large gardens, but every little helps.

top ten
insect food plants

- **Clovers and trefoils** many *Trifolium* and *Lotus* species

- **Docks and sorrels** many *Rumex* species, large and small

- **Gorse** *Ulex europaeus*

- **Grasses** (see the list of butterfly grasses on page 17)

- **Hop** *Humulus lupulus*

- **Lady's smock (cuckoo flower)** *Cardamine pratensis*

- **Pedunculate and sessile oaks** *Quercus robur and
  Q. petraea*

- **Stinging nettles** *Urtica dioica*

- **Thistles** many *Cirsium* and *Carduus* species

- **Sallows and willows** many *Salix* species and their cultivars

Feeding birds

A **bird-table or feeding station** is an easy way to attract a huge range of fascinating creatures, but there are a few basic rules.

- Site it in the open, where you can see it easily, and at least 2m from any tree or fence – too far for a cat to jump, but close enough to encourage timid birds.
- The higher off the ground the better.
- For best protection against weather and predators, use a roofed table.
- Opt for squirrel proof bird feeders.
- Fill hanging feeders with 'bird-safe' nuts, *not salted or roasted snacks*. Plastic mesh bags of nuts soon develop holes so a 5mm metal mesh hanger is better.
- Fruit, seeds, bird cake and nuts are good, but do not over-do kitchen scraps or bread products.

There are a wide choice of squirrel-proof bird feeders available and a variety of bird feeds. Peanuts are popular with many birds including the nuthatch (above) but try black sunflower seeds, fat balls or one of the many specialist mixes available to attract a variety of birds.

Hygiene

Clean bird tables and feeders regularly, remove rotting food and bird droppings to reduce the chance of any diseases being transmitted.

Ground feeding birds

Some, birds like blackbird, thrush, chaffinch, hedge sparrow and buntings, like to **feed on the ground**, but do not scatter large amounts of bread crust or kitchen scraps or you will only encourage mice and rats. A few seeds and berries are enough.

Water

Clean **drinking water is vital** for birds (and other wildlife). If you do not have a pond, a bird-bath will also attract drinking and splashing visitors. Alternatively, just put out bowls of fresh water. Think about those cats, though, when you decide where to place them.

Through the **seasons**

Winter is the most important time to feed birds, when natural food is scarce. However, the current recommendations are to feed all year – as long as nuts cannot be taken away whole. During the breeding season adults keep themselves going on nuts and seeds – giving them more energy to feed the chicks.

Avoid salty foods such as bacon rind and don't forget water and food for ground feeders. And if you find your garden under attack from caterpillars, what better organic remedy that hand picking the blighters and feeding them to the birds?

Opposite page: (top) blackbirds consume a varied diet, but prefer to feed on the ground; a greenfinch (middle) takes a bath and (bottom) spotted flycatcher parent and fledgling. Right: the acrobatic blue tit always provides good entertainment value.

35

House and home – a helping hand

If your garden is varied enough in its trees and plants, and you have enough hedges and creeper-covered fences, there will already be plenty of nest sites for birds. But you can always give a helping hand by putting up some nest boxes. Remember that birds value their privacy just as we do. A nest box in full view is less likely to attract tenants than one slightly hidden away in the undergrowth. Robins and wrens are renowned for nesting in peculiar places such as kettles, watering cans and flower pots, just as long as they are hidden from view.

Boxes and nests

A bird-box can be made from almost any wood: soft-wood, hard-wood, or MDF, which can be new or reclaimed. Most plywood is too thin – **12mm gives good insulation.** A sloping roof helps rain run off. Hinge it with a strip of roofing felt, rubber or flexible plastic so that it can easily be cleaned out at the end of each season. Include a **drainage** hole in the base.

Treat the **outside only** of the box with preservative (a low VOC water-based type) and allow time for residual smells to dissipate.

A young blue tit's first flight.

Box and nest sizes:

A standard box size for small birds like blue and great tit, sparrow and nuthatch is 15cm square and 20cm deep, with an entrance hole 25mm in diameter for blue and coal tits; 28mm for great tits and 32mm for sparrows and nuthatches.

Instead of a hole, leave the top half of the front wall open and birds like robin, wren, wagtails and blackbird will take up residence. A large box 20cm square and 45cm deep, with a hole 10cm x 15cm can house larger birds like starling, jackdaw, stock dove and perhaps even little owl or great spotted woodpecker. There is no need to line a box with dead leaves, grass, hay or straw, the birds prefer to furnish and feather their own nests.

House martins need a nest-cup under the eaves. Use half a coconut shell or mould one of about the same size out of clay or a cement/sawdust mixture using a child's ball to get the curvature. The entrance hole, cut into the rim, needs to be about 25mm deep.

Bats

A bat roost follows the standard bird box model, but instead of an entrance hole at the front, leave a 25mm gap at the back of the floor for them to crawl up into the box.

For successful occupancy, avoid disturbance to the birds or bats, put the boxes well up in trees, deep in bushes or in the dark middle of a thicket of climbers.

Tunnel vision

Dead tree trunks and stumps are far from dead as far as their visitors are concerned. As well as the deadwood-feeders, like stag beetle grubs, deep within, many bees and wasps use old woodworm tunnels in rotten wood, especially in a bright sunny position.

You can mimic a burrowed stump by drilling your own nesting holes into the wood. Bore

a variety of holes, 5-10mm in diameter, as deep as you can. Soon you will have leaf-cutter, carpenter and mason bees vying for position.

Mason bees normally burrow into the soft lime mortar of old walls, but modern concrete mortars are too tough. However mason bee kits are available to encourage these useful pollinators. They consist of a series of small cardboard tubes ready-made to attract nesting females.

Other bee nests can be made from bundles of bamboo canes, cut into short (15cm) lengths, or old bricks drilled through. Place them in a sunny place, by a wall.

Larger **mammals**

Many people think that to attract larger wildlife like foxes and badgers, you regularly have to put out food for them. There is nothing wrong with leaving out the occasional bowl of cat food or scraps, but although well-meaning, regular feeding creates problems by upsetting the local natural balance. Well-fed foxes successfully rear large litters of cubs. This increases the local population beyond what the area can truly sustain, increasing the spread of disease, damage to gardens and property, and any perceived 'pest' status.

action stations

1 **Plant** a variety of flowers, shrubs and trees to provide nectar, seeds, berries and nuts. Encourage any wild food plants for butterflies and other insects.

2 **Build** a bird table. Put out a variety of food including feeders stocked with nuts, seeds, breadcrumbs, berries and apples. Keep your bird table and feeding stations clean.

3 **Provide clean drinking water** which is vital to all wildlife. You don't need to have a pond – simply put out a clean supply in a bowl.

4 **Build or buy a home for wildlife:** Give a helping hand to birds by putting up some nest boxes. Drill nesting holes for insects into dead wood or even buy a nesting kit for mason bees.

4

Friends and foes

Friends and foes

Your wildlife garden will soon attract animals, especially smaller creatures like invertebrates, but some are easily misunderstood and wrongly seen as pests. Here is a gallery of frequently persecuted creatures that are, in fact, completely or mostly harmless.

Earwig (top), may nibble seedlings, but usually prefers already dead and decaying leaf matter. If they get too numerous make an earwig trap out of an upturned flower-pot stuffed with straw.

Woodlice (middle), much prefer dead and rotting plant material, but clear them out of the greenhouse.

Wasps (bottom), a useful predator that kills and eats flies, aphids and caterpillars. Most nests are well hidden and never a problem, but get professional help if you need one removed from an attic.

Hoverflies (top), often mistaken for stinging bees and wasps, but they are completely harmless. Many have voracious aphid-eating grubs too. All are strikingly pretty.

Cabbage whites (middle) only the large white, which lays clusters of eggs on the same leaf, does any real damage when its gregarious caterpillars ravage together. Small white and green-veined white caterpillars feed singly and secretively and so rarely do major harm.

Moths (bottom), sometimes regarded as sinister because they fly at night. Most feed on native plants in small numbers doing only little harm. Clothes-moths are tiny brown things, treat any indoors attack but leave the harmless species in the garden they are good bat food.

Garden snail. Will gnaw delicate-leaved plants, but mostly feeds on dead and decaying plant material. Avoid slug and snail pellets, or you may poison the thrushes and hedgehogs that prey on the snails. Instead, gather them into a bucket on a moist night and release them at a nearby wildlife site, woodland, railway embankment etc. (For more information on controlling slugs and snails naturally see *'Banish slugs'* in the Green Essentials series.

Mice. Mice can invade a compost bin if you use it for kitchen waste. Put the bin well away from the house. Start again if you find rats nesting inside.

Bats. They don't land on heads or get tangled in long hair, and they do not drink blood. They are wonderfully skilled aerial hunters of moths and they are declining nationally.

Keeping a **wildlife notebook**

You will soon realize how much wildlife there is in your garden, if you keep a regular diary or notebook. Record the plants and animals you see; when they first appear each year; what they are doing. If you record rainfall and temperature too, you can compare year-on-year notes and tally this with your wildlife observations.

Simply writing down the lists of plants, birds, insects and other animals will reinforce your knowledge, as you continually look up names and check information about their habits and behaviour. Your enthusiasm may even brush off onto friends and neighbours, encouraging them to think more about the wildlife they might have on their own doorsteps, but never noticed before.

Keep a lookout for the unusual. Waxwing consuming hawthorn berries (top); not all ladybirds are red, 14 spot ladybird (middle) and the harmless grass snake (recorded in 4% of gardens).

Lookout stations

Keep a lookout for creatures you have specifically planted and designed for. Thistles and cardoons are a favourite with goldfinches, golden rod sprays are perfect hoverfly magnets, figworts are visited almost exclusively by wasps. If you let that grass grow long, look out for butterflies including the small skipper. Take a look under the stones you put round the pond, you may find overwintering newts, frogs and toads. And listen out for the thwack of snail-shell on boulder as a thrush uses one for its anvil.

Garden **BirdWatch**

There are over 16,000 Garden BirdWatch lookout stations in the UK, where wildlife enthusiasts record the birds and animals they see. **Did you know?**

- Blackbirds, blue tits and robins are all found in more than 90% of gardens

- The number of goldfinches visiting gardens each winter is rising dramatically. The great news is that it has recently been taken off the list of species of conservation concern.

- House sparrows, which are declining in number rapidly in many areas, feed their chicks on aphids during the first few days of life – which is great news for gardeners.

▌ *Above: (left) house sparrows and (right) bullfinch both on the decline in many areas.*

- In a Garden BirdWatch survey, the most common wild mammal to be seen was the grey squirrel, which visited 67% of gardens. Hedgehog was second (40%).

- 64% of gardens were visited by frogs and 28% by toads. Grass snakes were found in 4%.

- The most common butterflies were red admiral (65%), peacock (56%) and small tortoiseshell (55%).

- Blackbirds nesting in gardens are more successful than those which nest in farmland and woodland, despite the presence of more cats.

Why not get involved in Garden BirdWatch? You will learn more about the birds and animals visiting your garden and you will be helping to keep an eye on Britain's wildlife. *For a free enquiry pack*, write to Attracting Wildlife, Garden BirdWatch, The Nunnery, Thetford, Norfolk, IP24 2PU or visit www.bto.org/gbw

Resources

Useful addresses, contacts and further information

British Trust for Ornithology (BTO), The Nunnery, Thetford, Norfolk, IP24 2PU. The British Trust for Ornithology organizes the popular all-year Garden BirdWatch survey, together with a variety of other national bird surveys. **www.bto.org**

Butterfly Conservation, Manor Yard, East Lulworth, Wareham, Dorset BH20 5QP runs a garden butterfly survey each year and produces a *Gardens for butterflies* pack. **www.butterfly-conservation.org**

English Nature, Northminster House, Peterborough PE1 1UA.
Advises government on nature conservation in England. Produces numerous useful publications including: *Wildlife-friendly gardening*, a general guide, which is available on-line. **www.english-nature.org.uk**

Henry Doubleday Research Association. National Centre for Organic Gardening, Ryton-on-Dunsmore, Coventry CV8 3LG. Researches and promotes organic gardening. Publishes many helpful books, leaflets and factsheets, including *Flowers for the wildlife garden* which is available on-line. **www.hdra.org.uk**

Plantlife International, The Wild-Plant Conservation Charity, 14 Rollestone Street, Salisbury,. Wiltshire SP1 1DX. **www.plantlife.org.uk**

Royal Society for the Protection of Birds (RSPB), The Lodge, Sandy, Bedfordshire SG19 2DL. **www.rspb.org.uk**

The Wildlife Trusts, The Kiln, Waterside, Mather Road, Newark, Nottinghamshire NG24 1WT. A partnership of all the local wildlife trusts publish various leaflets on urban and garden animals **www.wildlifetrusts.org**. With New Holland Publishers the Wildlife Trusts have produced several books including: *The Wildlife Trusts guide to garden wildlife* edited by N. Hammond, *The garden bird handbook: how to attract, identify and watch the birds in your garden* by Stephen Moss, *Back garden nature reserve* by Chris Packham. **www.newhollandpublishers.com**